D1266972

Garden in My Heart

POEM FLOWERS OF FAITH AND FRIENDSHIP

Garden in My Heart

BY

JAMES J. METCALFE

AUTHOR OF

"POEM PORTRAITS"

Garden City Books

GARDEN CITY, NEW YORK

Nihil obstat
JOHN M. A. FEARNS, S.T.D.
Censor Librorum

Imprimatur
✠FRANCIS CARDINAL SPELLMAN,
Archbishop of New York

New York, February 4, 1949

Printed in the United States
at
The Country Life Press, Garden City, N. Y.

Dedication

I dedicate this book to God . . . And to the Holy See . . . To Mary and St. Joseph and . . . To all who pray for me . . . I hope each little thought in rhyme . . . Will reach around the earth . . . To help inspire other souls . . . To be of better worth . . . To comfort all the lonely who . . . Are given to despair . . . And lift the ones so weary with . . . The burden they must bear . . . May every message serve at last . . . To take some tear away . . . And add a bit of sunshine to . . . The passing of the day . . . That all the world may recognize . . . Our Lord and Saviour true . . . And as we live our hearts may give . . . The homage He is due.

Preface

Ever since he began writing his syndicated newspaper feature, "Portraits," James J. Metcalfe has realized that his poetic ability is a gift from God and that it was given him to use for the joy and encouragement of his fellow beings.

That is why for many years now he has been devoting his Sunday column to prayer or other religious theme. It is his way of giving gratitude to God.

More recently, and aside from his daily Portraits, Mr. Metcalfe undertook the writing of special prayer-poems at the invitation of Frank Quin & Co. of Philadelphia, which distributed them in lithographed card form. These holy and friendly thoughts proved so popular that it was decided to publish them as a permanent collection.

Those who have read the author's recent book, *Poem Portraits,* need no introduction to James Metcalfe—poet, journalist, lawyer, lecturer and former FBI man. Born in Berlin, Germany, on September 16, 1906, he received his early education at the University of Notre Dame and his law degree from Loyola University, Chicago. Devoted husband and father of three children, he is a deeply religious family man. His sincere interest in the little things of everyday living as expressed in his appealing Portraits has won him admirers around the world.

Today the thoughts of James Metcalfe appear in some 100 newspapers in the United States and in Canada and Ireland. Yet he derives his profoundest gratification from his ability to write these special prayer-poems that lift the heart to God and provide a source of lasting inspiration. Truly they are gems of religious wisdom . . . poem flowers of faith and friendship.

The Publishers

Contents

THE TEN COMMANDMENTS

Garden in My Heart

I have a garden in my heart . . . Where friendly flowers grow . . . And each one has the gentle name . . . Of somebody I know . . . Their petals are the memories . . . Of passing smiles and tears . . . Their stems are sturdy shafts of love . . . That last throughout the years . . . I tend my garden carefully . . . And keep its beauty bright . . . Beneath a kindly sun by day . . . And faithful stars at night . . . The wind may blow, the snow may fall . . . The rain may gather gloom . . . But in the garden of my heart . . . The flowers always bloom . . . I do not ever pluck them for . . . The vases on my shelves . . . Because I know they would not last . . . Or multiply themselves.

Be with Me Always

Dear God, be with me when the day . . . Is beautiful and bright . . . And when the silver stars reflect . . . The glory of the night . . . When clouds are gathering and when . . . The sky begins to rain . . . And every time I am inclined . . . To murmur or complain . . . In sorrow and in happiness . . . And all the hours long . . . And when temptation faces me . . . And I am not so strong . . . Be with me, God, to keep me well . . . And to encourage me . . . That I may give my best to each . . . Responsibility . . . And when at last my name is called . . . And I must go from here . . . Please take me in Your arms, dear God . . . And still my every fear.

Success in Life

There are a thousand ways to gain . . . The glory of success . . . But only those are worth our while . . . That bring us happiness . . . The peace of mind that promises . . . The joy of heart and soul . . . Because our purpose is to reach . . . A good and worthy goal . . . There is no profit to be had . . . In just possessing things . . . And gathering the diamonds . . . Of gold and silver rings . . . Or building up a power that . . . Would rule the world some day . . . Until all human liberties . . . Must fall and fade away . . . There is no other key in life . . . To genuine success . . . Except to open every door . . . To lasting happiness.

The Sacred Heart

Wherever you may go in life . . . Whatever you may do . . . May you be with the Sacred Heart . . . And may It be with you . . . May all Its grace and blessing and . . . Its peace be in your soul . . . And may Its merits plead for you . . . To help you to your goal . . . May you be fervent as the flames . . . That fill the Sacred Heart . . . And may Its sorrows comfort you . . . Whenever dreams depart . . . May you be always zealous as . . . The Sacred Heart has been . . . And may Its virtues shine for you . . . To conquer every sin . . . May you approach the Sacred Heart . . . With love and reverence . . . And may the Blessed Vision be . . . Your lasting recompense.

O Virgin Mary

O Mary, Queen of Heaven and . . . Of all the angels there . . . I beg of you to listen to . . . My very special prayer . . . I need your intercession and . . . In this my fervent plea . . . I call your name a thousand times . . . Upon my rosary . . . I say The Memorare and . . . I know that it is true . . . And that is why I fold my hands . . . And bow my head to you . . . O Virgin Mary, Mother dear . . . By every virtue blest . . . Please ask your Son, Our Lord and God . . . To grant this one request . . . Look not upon my sinful soul . . . But hear my humble heart . . . That I may put away the past . . . And make a nobler start.

Help Us, St. Joseph

O good St. Joseph, in your name . . . We ask for grace and light . . . To live a better life each day . . . By doing what is right . . . Inspire us to holiness . . . And virtue unashamed . . . Instill in us the zeal with which . . . Your spirit is inflamed . . . Watch over us in happiness . . . And when our hopes are dim . . . Protect us from all harm and hurt . . . As you protected Him . . . O good and kind St. Joseph, be . . . Our foster-father too . . . And let us bring our problems and . . . Our troubled hearts to you . . . Teach us to work for Jesus Christ . . . With every deed and breath . . . Help us to live a holy life . . . And die a happy death.

Dear Guardian Angel

Dear Guardian Angel, take my hand . . . And guide me through the day . . . That I may walk the proper path . . . And never go astray . . . Let not the smallest sinful thought . . . Be present in my mind . . . Let not my tongue say idle things . . . Or utter words unkind . . . Inspire me with bravery . . . To overcome all odds . . . And help me hear and understand . . . The teachings that are God's . . . Protect my heart from prejudice . . . And keep my body well . . . That I may give the best in me . . . And constantly excel . . . Dear Guardian Angel, lead me through . . . The darkness of the night . . . And let my eyes behold The Star . . . Of Everlasting Light.

Above the Clouds

When I am soaring in a plane . . . Above the clouds of white . . . I seem to touch the dawn and feel . . . The majesty of night . . . . I see the rolling earth below . . . And it appears to me . . . That all the world is just a speck . . . In God's infinity . . . It makes me understand how small . . . We human beings are . . . No larger than the naked eye . . . . Beholds a tiny star . . . And then I see the emptiness . . . Of avarice and greed . . . And why our faithfulness to God . . . Is what we really need . . . And why we should not be content . . . With any worldly goal . . . But only how we honor Him . . . And sanctify the soul.

The Deed Means More

Our prayers and good intentions have . . . A special place on earth . . . And every kindly thought we think . . . Is not without its worth . . . But what is more important is . . . The deed we do each day . . . In friendship unto others and . . . To help them on their way . . . The actual accomplishment . . . Of something good and true . . . That may enable other souls . . . To see their struggles through . . . For that is why almighty God . . . Created everyone . . . And why He filled the night with stars . . . And set the morning sun . . . So we would really give our all . . . For human happiness . . . Instead of merely saying prayers . . . And making promises.

Little Child's Prayer

Dear Lord, I hope this day will be . . . A happy one for You and me . . . I hope I do not make You sad . . . By doing something that is bad . . . I want to be real good to You . . . The way my parents teach me to . . . Because, dear Lord, I love You so . . . For helping me to learn and grow . . . For being kind to me each day . . . And watching when I sleep or play . . . Please listen to my little prayer . . . And keep me in Your loving care . . . I never want to make You cry . . . Or spoil the sunshine in the sky . . . I only want to look above . . . And give You happiness and love.

Joyous Feast

O Heart of Gold, I need not wish . . . A better life for you . . . Because you have enough to make . . . Your wishes all come true . . . I need not pray for sunshine or . . . The clouds to go away . . . As long as you are brave enough . . . To meet the coming day . . . God made you just as generous . . . As you could ever be . . . And all your happiness is in . . . Your love and sympathy . . . O Heart of Gold, your path is one . . . Of glory and of pride . . . While there is everlasting light . . . And Christ is at your side . . . Behold the splendid majesty . . . The angels now unfold . . . And give yourself for evermore . . . To God, O Heart of Gold.

My First Communion

Dear Lord, I am so little to . . . Receive my first Communion . . . And yet I think I understand . . . The meaning of this union . . . The miracle of meeting You . . . And knowing You are present . . . To give me holiness and grace . . . And comfort sweet and pleasant . . . This pure and ever spotless host . . . The priest has consecrated . . . Your precious Body and Your Blood . . . For which my soul has waited . . . I bend my knees in humbleness . . . And bow my head before You . . . And with my young and loving heart . . . Sincerely I adore You . . . O dear Lord Jesus, come to me . . . In this my first Communion . . . And grant my wish that ours will be . . . An everlasting union.

The Good in Us

There is some good in each of us . . . However bad we seem . . . And everybody has at least . . . One truly noble dream . . . We may succumb to circumstance . . . Or we may simply stray . . . And we may shun the golden chance . . . That seldom comes our way . . . But each and every one of us . . . Has some redeeming trait . . . That could be used to save our souls . . . Before it is too late . . . And that is strictly up to us . . . And we must make the choice . . . For we are not the lowly slaves . . . Of any hand or voice . . . We have the freedom of our will . . . And God is on our side . . . If only we are brave enough . . . To tackle every tide.

By the Grace of God

My soul belongs to God because . . . He gave my soul to me . . . And it is His to have and hold . . . For all eternity . . . And therefore I must do my best . . . To keep it white and pure . . . However great the struggle He . . . May want me to endure . . . However dark the shadows or . . . The fury of the rain . . . Or any other reason for . . . A creature to complain . . . I must remember always that . . . He placed me here on earth . . . And I must have His guiding grace . . . To be of any worth . . . No matter if I win at once . . . Or wearily I plod . . . In every dream and every deed . . . My soul belongs to God.

God, Bless Our Home

God, bless this home in which we live . . . Protect its every wall . . . And let no evil enter and . . . No tragedy befall . . . Let not the loudest storm prevail . . . Against the chimney-place . . . But keep us safe beneath the roof . . . Of Your eternal grace . . . Let stars adorn each window-pane . . . And sunbeams light the floor . . . And grant that only friendly hands . . . May knock upon our door . . . God, bless our home with happiness . . . And loving thoughts of You . . . And while Your holy will be done . . . May all our dreams come true . . . Be with us when we greet the dawn . . . And when we take our rest . . . And every moment in our home . . . Be our beloved Guest.

O Infant Jesus of Prague

O Infant Jesus, sweet and mild . . . We lift our eyes to You . . . O holy little King of Prague . . . We promise to be true . . . In Your resplendent robe and crown . . . You rule the land and sea . . . While in Your hand You hold the world . . . And all its destiny . . . You give Your blessings to the ones . . . Who honor You today . . . As surely as Your heart is grieved . . . By those who go astray . . . O gently little Majesty . . . We bow before Your feet . . . And reverently invoke Your name . . . While humbly we entreat . . . O Infant Jesus, let us share . . . The blessings You bestow . . . That we may tell Your miracles . . . For everyone to know.

My Prayer Book

I try to find the proper words . . . Whenever I would pray . . . But I can never think of those . . . That I would like to say . . . And that is why I always have . . . My prayer book at my side . . . Because its every printed page . . . Provides a perfect guide . . . It tells me how to turn to God . . . And ask Him for His aid . . . And give my gratitude to Him . . . When I have made the grade . . . Its paragraphs express my thoughts . . . And help me to confess . . . The sins that might deprive me of . . . Eternal happiness . . . My prayer book is the faithful friend . . . I carry everywhere . . . So I may talk to God with all . . . The beauty of a prayer.

On Your Wedding Day

God bless you on your wedding day . . . With all the grace to be . . . The wife and husband who will live . . . In love and sympathy . . . For better or for worse in life . . . Of virtue and of wealth . . . For richer or for poorer and . . . In sickness or in health . . . May you be tolerant and kind . . . And grateful for each joy . . . And may you have the blessing of . . . A baby girl or boy . . . May all your anniversaries . . . Have happiness to hold . . . With kisses, dreams and memories . . . Of silver and of gold . . . In holy matrimony you . . . Are joined by hand and heart . . . God bless you on your wedding day . . . And never let you part.

I Trust in God

I trust in God with all my heart . . . Because I know that He . . . Is my divine Creator and . . . He gave my life to me . . . He made the body I possess . . . And blessed me with a mind . . . To study and to understand . . . Whatever I may find . . . He watches over me each day . . . And when I sleep at night . . . And as I follow in His path . . . I see His guiding light . . . I trust in God implicitly . . . For everything I need . . . And dedicate to Him each prayer . . . And suffering and deed . . . Because His heavenly reward . . . Is my eternal goal . . . And in my homage to my God . . . I hope to save my soul.

Priest

The priest is more than just a man . . . Who walks and eats and drinks . . . He is the image of Our Lord . . . In what he says and thinks . . . He is a creature set apart . . . From all the world of sin . . . To guide us in the game of life . . . And show us how to win . . . His fingers are anointed so . . . That they may touch The Host . . . And bless us for The Father and . . . The Son and Holy Ghost . . . To help us and forgive us when . . . We fall away from grace . . . To marry us, baptize us and . . . Protect our resting-place . . . The priest is one who gladly gives . . . His life for you and me . . . That we may share the golden joy . . . Of God's eternity.

Nun

She sacrifices luxury . . . To spend her nights and days . . . In folds of queenly poverty . . . Beyond our worldly ways . . . She lives a life of charity . . . With every deed a prayer . . . For all the large and little souls . . . Entrusted to her care . . . The poor and humble and the rich . . . The feeble, blind and lame . . . The ones who never heard of God . . . And those who say His name . . . Her time is His and it belongs . . . To all the world He made . . . Wherever she is needed most . . . And she can be of aid . . . Her heart goes out to everyone . . . Wherever voices call . . . Especially the children who . . . Cling tightly to her shawl.

Visit to the Church

I love the Catholic church because . . . I know that every day . . . Its doors are always open and . . . I may go in and pray . . . I know that I may enter there . . . And occupy a pew . . . To kneel or sit and fold my hands . . . The way all Catholics do . . . Or I may seek the altar rail . . . And light a candle there . . . And drop a little offering . . . To emphasize my prayer . . . The church is strangely silent when . . . I am in there alone . . . And yet it holds the greatest peace . . . That I have ever known . . . Because my everlasting God . . . Is present night and day . . . To read my thoughts and listen to . . . Whatever words I say.

Thank You, Queen Mary

Dear Mother Mary, Queen of all . . . The earth and sky above . . . I offer you my gratitude . . . And everlasting love . . . My gratitude for every gift . . . That you have given me . . . And my affection for your grace . . . And boundless sympathy . . . You have inspired me to do . . . My utmost every day . . . To honor God and live my life . . . According to His way . . . Your name is always on my lips . . . Your picture in my heart . . . And you are every masterpiece . . . Of beauty and of art . . . O Mary, Queen of all the world . . . I have no cause to fear . . . As long as you are at my side . . . To help me persevere.

Trial on Earth

The time we spend upon this earth . . . Is little more or less . . . Than something to determine our . . . Degree of willingness . . . It is the trial period when . . . Our selfishness is weighed . . . To test our human competence . . . And give us each a grade . . . Because the day will come when we . . . Must stand before God's throne . . . And in that final hour we . . . Shall find ourselves alone . . . No counsel and no witnesses . . . Will come to plead our case . . . For we ourselves will have to prove . . . That we have earned our place . . . And wealth or fame will matter not . . . Or any pain or ache . . . But only how we tried to live . . . For someone else's sake.

God Forgive Me

May God forgive me for the sins . . . That weigh my weary soul . . . And for my frequent failure to . . . Perform a better role . . . May He be merciful to me . . . Instead of being just . . . When I have spent my span on earth . . . And I return to dust . . . I know I am not worthy of . . . The blessings He would give . . . And maybe there are times when I . . . Do not deserve to live . . . But in my wilderness I kneel . . . And make my plea to Him . . . Whose love is just as gentle as . . . His vengeance may be grim . . . That He will lead me by the hand . . . To my eternal goal . . . And He will take away the sins . . . That weigh my weary soul.

Faith and Purpose

However dark the day may seem . . . Or steep the path I plod . . . I have no fear because I know . . . I have my faith in God . . . I know He will not leave me or . . . Forget me in my need . . . As long as I believe in Him . . . With every thought and deed . . . I may be foolish now and then . . . And I may lose the way . . . But He is always at my side . . . Wherever I may stray . . . His guiding grace reminds me of . . . The mercy He has shown . . . And in my deepest misery . . . I never feel alone . . . I know my God is willing to . . . Forgive my every sin . . . As long as I have faith and I . . . Sincerely try to win.

Notre Dame

The golden dome of Notre Dame . . . Reflects the friendly sky . . . To symbolize the warmth and love . . . That keep her spirit high . . . And there Our Lady reaches out . . . As though to bless the earth . . . Where men prepare their inner selves . . . To be of greater worth . . . The gentlemen of Notre Dame . . . Who face whatever odds . . . And who devoutly understand . . . The glory that is God's . . . Our Lady gazes joyfully . . . On all her faithful sons . . . And lavishes her loving grace . . . Upon the priests and nuns . . . Her graduates may walk alone . . . Or they may rise to fame . . . But in their humble hearts they all . . . Belong to Notre Dame.

Prayer at Benediction

O Holy Host! My Lord and God! . . . I kneel before Your throne . . . Let me receive the grace divine . . . That comes from You alone . . . Bestow on me Your blessing in . . . This hour of my need . . . And help me consecrate to You . . . My every word and deed . . . On bended knee I bow my head . . . And silently I pray . . . That Your dear benediction will . . . Be with me every day . . . I love You and adore You and . . . I praise Your Holy Name . . . With all the zeal and fervor of . . . An everlasting flame . . . O Holy Host! Look down on me . . . From Your majestic height . . . And with Your blessing make my soul . . . More worthy in Your sight.

Way of the Cross

Dear Lord, when I am weary and . . . My life appears a loss . . . I follow in Your footsteps to . . . The Stations of The Cross . . . I hear Your Name condemned to death . . . I see Your journey start . . . Beneath a crown of cruel thorns . . . And sorrow in Your Heart . . . I watch You fall beneath Your Cross . . . And struggle to arise . . . And I behold the tears that fill . . . Your Mother's loving eyes . . . I hear the hammer and I see . . . Your Body crucified . . . And when the lance has pierced Your Heart . . . I know that You have died . . . And then I put away my thoughts . . . Of weariness and pain . . . For I am too ashamed, dear Lord . . . To murmur or complain.

My Christmas Wish

I hope the little Heart of Him . . . Who is our little King . . . Will bless you on this Christmas Day . . . And bring you everything . . . The Heart that loves us even when . . . It seems so all alone . . . And though It is a tiny Heart . . . Is greater than our own . . . I hope His Blessed Mother with . . . Her eyes of heaven-blue . . . Will be your inspiration and . . . Your every dream come true . . . May good St. Joseph pray for you . . . And in his gentle way . . . Fulfill my wish of happiness . . . For you on Christmas Day . . . I pray that you may always please . . . The Holy Family . . . And share the comfort of their peace . . . For all eternity.

Miracles Happen

A miracle can happen but . . . It takes the strong belief . . . Of confidence to overcome . . . The most enduring grief . . . A mountain may be moved by faith . . . If we sincerely try . . . And we may even change the clouds . . . And color of the sky . . . But first and last it all depends . . . On God's eternal way . . . And whether we fulfill the vows . . . We make from day to day . . . We have to pray with courage and . . . The strength of heart and mind . . . To leave our tribulations and . . . Our miseries behind . . . And then if we are honest and . . . Our sentiments are right . . . The greatest miracle on earth . . . May happen overnight.

Good Morning, God

Good morning, God, and thank You for . . . The glory of the sun . . . And thank You for the health I have . . . To get my duty done . . . I shall devote the hours of . . . This golden day to You . . . By honoring Your holy name . . . In everything I do . . . I shall pursue my daily art . . . Without complaint or fear . . . And spend my every effort to . . . Be friendly and sincere . . . I know there have been many days . . . That I have whiled away . . . But this is one that I will try . . . To make Your special day . . . And so once more, good morning, God . . . And please depend on me . . . Because I want to honor You . . . For all eternity.

Good Night, O Lord

Before I go to sleep, O Lord . . . I want to say this prayer . . . That You will always keep me in . . . Your kind and loving care . . . That You will let my body rest . . . And let my mind relax . . . And fill my dreams with holy thoughts . . . Instead of wordly facts . . . I ask that You forgive me for . . . My failures of today . . . And give me all the grace I need . . . To live a better way . . . Watch over me tonight, O Lord . . . And in my heart instill . . . The fervor and the constancy . . . To do Your holy will . . . I want to follow You and grow . . . More worthy in Your sight . . . O Lord, please listen to my prayer . . . And hear me say good night.

His Will Be Done

How can a soul deny its God . . . Or ever put away . . . The miracles of life and time . . . That happen every day? . . . How can a creature on this earth . . . Be confident and sure . . . When only by the will of God . . . The body may endure? . . . There is no thought or word or scheme . . . Nor any song to sing . . . Except as God allows the world . . . And governs everything . . . He made the flowers and the trees . . . The fertile fields that grow . . . He set the stars, the moon and sun . . . And let the rivers flow . . . His heart is filled with mercy and . . . His gaze is sweetly sad . . . He blesses those who love Him and . . . He punishes the bad.

For My Friends

I thank You, God, sincerely for . . . The friends I have today . . . And all that they have done for me . . . To help me on my way . . . I thank You that I met them in . . . Good fellowship and cheer . . . And that in time of need or stress . . . They always have been near . . . The friends who have inspired me . . . To make another gain . . . However loud the thunder or . . . Discouraging the rain . . . I thank You for my faithful friends . . . In places near and far . . . Whose kindly deeds have made my days . . . As fruitful as they are . . . Whose happy songs have done so much . . . To make my dreams come true . . . And who by their example, God . . . Have drawn me close to You.

St. Patrick to All

We honor you, St. Patrick, for . . . The patriarch you are . . . And for the constant guidance of . . . Your bright and shining star . . . You banished all the evil snakes . . . From Ireland's sunny shore . . . And brought eternal faith in God . . . To every Irish door . . . And now your holy fame has spread . . . Beyond the seven seas . . . And legion are the converts who . . . Present their fervent pleas . . . The shamrock is the symbol of . . . Your everlasting worth . . . That reaches every corner of . . . This pleasure-seeking earth . . . There is no final shoreline and . . . There is no solid wall . . . Because as Ireland's patron saint . . . Your name is loved by all.

My Time on Earth

The time is long when I have let . . . The hours slip away . . . Without a single kindly deed . . . To occupy the day . . . When I have been a selfish soul . . . From morning until night . . . With never any thought or word . . . To make the heavens bright . . . But when I strive to do my best . . . For others on this earth . . . I feel my humble efforts are . . . Of some enduring worth . . . And then the moments seem to fly . . . And life itself is brief . . . As I extend a helping hand . . . To those who gather grief . . . And so I know I should not waste . . . One minute of the day . . . That might inspire other souls . . . And help them on their way.

I Love My God

I love my God because He is . . . My Master and my King . . . And He is kind, considerate . . . And fair in everything . . . He blest me with the breath to live . . . A mind to think and dream . . . And with the hands to carry out . . . The task of every scheme . . . He gave me ears with which to hear . . . Each word and every sound . . . My feet to walk and eyes to see . . . The beauty all around . . . I have the sense of smelling and . . . A tongue with which to speak . . . And all the freedom of my will . . . For every goal I seek . . . I love my God for all the gifts . . . That He has given me . . . And that is why I always try . . . To serve Him faithfully.

Visit the Sick

A visit to the sick is such . . . A brief and little thing . . . And, yet, consider all the joy . . . And good that it can bring . . . It means so much in every way . . . To one who lies in bed . . . With only flowers to observe . . . And papers to be read . . . A visit gives that human touch . . . Of one more helping hand . . . And all the faithful friendliness . . . That tries to understand . . . Indeed The Lord Himself has said . . . That we are serving Him . . . Each time we help some lonely soul . . . In moments dark or dim . . . So let us pay a visit to . . . Our neighbors in their pain . . . And magnify the rainbow bright . . . That glorifies the rain.

Voice of God

The voice of God is never loud . . . Or painful to the ear . . . And though we are inclined to stray . . . It is forever near . . . It is a calm and gentle voice . . . That whispers to the heart . . . And counsels us to weigh the world . . . And choose the better part . . . When we are lost in loneliness . . . And when the day is dim . . . It calls to us with loving tone . . . And beckons us to Him . . . And when we are successful and . . . We feel a certain pride . . . It cautions us to try to keep . . . A humble heart inside . . . The voice of God is all we need . . . To guide us on our way . . . If we are given faithfully . . . To listen and obey.

My Daily Offering

O Jesus, through Your Mother's heart . . . I offer You today . . . My prayers and works and sufferings . . . And all I do or say . . . I offer You the picture of . . . My hopes and fantasies . . . My dreams of some tomorrow and . . . My dearest memories . . . The sunshine and the shadows and . . . The smiles and tears of life . . . Its triumphs and its pleasures and . . . Its struggle and its strife . . . I offer You my heart and soul . . . My hands and feet and eyes . . . And all the faculties I have . . . Without the least disguise . . . And with repentance for my sins . . . I promise I will do . . . My faithful best for evermore . . . To serve and honor You.

God's Family

The family belongs to God . . . In quite a special way . . . And it should dedicate itself . . . To Jesus every day . . . The father and the mother and . . . The little girl or boy . . . Who live together and who share . . . Each sorrow and each joy . . . Who dream their dreams of happiness . . . And plan the years ahead . . . The while they struggle patiently . . . To earn their daily bread . . . They are the special choice of God . . . For blessings rich and bright . . . If only they will pray to Him . . . Each morning and each night . . . If only they will honor Him . . . And do their best to be . . . As humble and devoted as . . . The Holy Family.

Sign of the Cross

The sign of the Cross is my only sign . . . Wherever I go in life . . . The special sign that is always mine . . . To conquer the strongest strife . . . Whatever the duty that must be done . . . I say it again and again . . . "In the name of The Father and of The Son . . . And The Holy Ghost—Amen" . . . I make the sign of the Cross at dawn . . . When the sky is a golden gleam . . . And after the glory of day is gone . . . In the star of a silver dream . . . I never look back and I never care . . . For the world that I used to know . . . As long as the sign of the Cross is there . . . To show me the way to go . . . I wander the waves of the wildest sea . . . With never an albatross . . . For the grace of God is a part of me . . . In the sign of the Holy Cross.

Hail, Holy Queen

O hail to you, our Holy Queen . . . O gentle Mother Mary . . . Our life, our sweetness and our hope . . . Wherever we may tarry . . . To you we banished children cry . . . With mourning and with weeping . . . That we may leave this vale of tears . . . And nestle in your keeping . . . Turn, then, most gracious advocate . . . Your eyes in our direction . . . And sanctify us with the grace . . . Of your divine perfection . . . And after this our exile show . . . The Child you used to carry . . . O clement, sweet and loving and . . . Most holy Virgin Mary . . . O wondrous Mother of Our Lord . . . Bestow your prayerful token . . . So we may earn the promises . . . That Jesus Christ has spoken.

Prayer for the Church

O God, our refuge and our strength . . . Look down on us today . . . As we Your people cry to you . . . And fervently we pray . . . Through holy Mother Mary and . . . Her spouse, St. Joseph too . . . And blessed Paul and Peter we . . . Present our plea to You . . . In mercy and in goodness hear . . . The prayer we now exclaim . . . That sinners may repent their wrongs . . . And praise Your Holy Name . . . Exalt our holy mother Church . . . And grant that she may be . . . Enriched by recognition and . . . Secure in liberty . . . O God, give us the help we ask . . . A thousand times again . . . With humble and adoring hearts . . . Through Christ our Lord—Amen.

Prayer to St. Michael

O holy Michael, guard us now . . . Against the way of sin . . . Inspire us with courage and . . . The strength we need to win . . . Defend us in our battle to . . . Destroy the devil's snares . . . And to defeat his malice with . . . Our efforts and our prayers . . . Let not his wickedness prevail . . . In any thought or deed . . . Or any tempting word that speaks . . . Of selfishness and greed . . . Archangel Michael, may you come . . . With your celestial host . . . To help us in this hour when . . . We mortals need you most . . . And by the power that is God's . . . Cast Satan into hell . . . With all the evil spirits we . . . Are striving to dispel.

The Lord Is Lonely

The Lord is always lonely when . . . We do not say a prayer . . . To let Him know that in our hearts . . . We have not ceased to care . . . However busy we may be . . . With plans and problems grim . . . He always likes to hear that we . . . Have not forgotten Him . . . Because a little prayer is such . . . An easy thing to say . . . It only takes a minute of . . . An hour in the day . . . It is the least that we can do . . . To show that we believe . . . And give our gratitude for all . . . The blessings we receive . . . The Lord is always lonely in . . . The love He longs to share . . . Unless we keep Him company . . . By whispering a prayer.

Kind Word

A word of kindness does so much . . . When it is really meant . . . And though it is a world of wealth . . . It does not cost a cent . . . It is the key of friendship that . . . Unlocks the strangest door . . . And it promotes the partnership . . . That lasts for evermore . . . It overcomes a sudden wrath . . . And calms the troubled mind . . . It generates eternal hope . . . And leaves despair behind . . . A little word of kindness is . . . A sort of magic way . . . To manufacture sunshine when . . . The sky is dull and gray . . . It does not take much effort and . . . It brings its own reward . . . If only in the fact that it . . . Is pleasing to The Lord.

O Pray for Me!

God knows my heart and all the skies . . . Are overcast today . . . Because the holy angels came . . . To take your soul away . . . But I am happy in the thought . . . That you are there with Him . . . Where joy is everlasting and . . . The light is never dim . . . I say a thousand prayers that send . . . Indulgences to you . . . Although I know your loving soul . . . Could only need a few . . . And now that you are saintly and . . . From sin forever free . . . I hope with all my heart that you . . . Will intercede for me . . . For I am so unworthy and . . . There is so much I owe . . . That I need all the grace that God . . . Is willing to bestow.

Praise Be to God

Praise be to God for all the things . . . That comfort us today . . . Good health, a song of happiness . . . And friends along the way . . . A home that we may call our own . . . However small and bare . . . Eternal opportunity . . . And freedom from despair . . . Sufficient food and clothing and . . . The luxuries of life . . . And all the wisdom and the strength . . . To conquer every strife . . . We may not do the best we can . . . And we may not succeed . . . But we have all the implements . . . That we could ever need . . . And we have faith and hope and so . . . Our humble hearts should say . . . Praise be to God for all the things . . . That comfort us today.

Little Men

When God designed the universe . . . And made the world and when . . . He fashioned souls, He must have loved . . . And blessed the little men . . . The little men who work each day . . . To earn their daily bread . . . And think about their families . . . Before they go to bed . . . Who never reach for worldly wealth . . . Or look around for fame . . . But who are satisfied to have . . . An ordinary name . . . Because He made so many and . . . They are His counterpart . . . In kindness and devotion and . . . Sincerity of heart . . . He must have always loved and blest . . . The little men on earth . . . Because their humbleness reflects . . . Their everlasting worth.

Safe with St. Christopher

When I am traveling on foot . . . Or when I chance to ride . . . I always have St. Christopher . . . Securely at my side . . . Because I know that he will keep . . . My body safe and sound . . . Whenever I am flying or . . . I journey on the ground . . . He watches over me at home . . . And in the strangest place . . . Especially when I approach . . . A danger I must face . . . He guides and guards me faithfully . . . Wherever I may go . . . As once he helped a child to cross . . . The river's raging flow . . . I never take the smallest step . . . Or sail the calmest sea . . . Unless I have my medal of . . . St. Christopher with me.

Father's Prayer

O God, look down upon our home . . . With kind and gentle eyes . . . And pour Your blessings great and small . . . Upon our family ties . . . Be good to her, my loving wife . . . Who is so good to me . . . And help me honor You and her . . . With love and loyalty . . . Bestow on us the guiding grace . . . We need from day to day . . . To raise our children properly . . . At home and church and play . . . We trust in you with all our hearts . . . And offer you our prayers . . . Our smiles and tears, our glories and . . . Our little daily cares . . . We thank You, God, for everything . . . Beneath the stars and sun . . . And promise we will always strive . . . To help Your will be done.

Let Me Not Hate

God, give me warmth of heart and soul . . . To live a better way . . . And add a bit of sunshine bright . . . To some-one else's day . . . Let me not hate my neighbor or . . . Despise my enemy . . . But help me to be good to all . . . With love and sympathy . . . I want to be of service and . . . To do my humble part . . . To foster faith and hope anew . . . In every human heart . . . I long to live unselfishly . . . In patience and in prayer . . . And give the best there is in me . . . To people everywhere . . . God, let me not forget this aim . . . And never let me hate . . . But guide me to eternal joy . . . Be-yond Your golden gate.

Faith of a Child

One day when I went into church . . . I saw a little child . . . Who knelt before the altar rail . . . And very sweetly smiled . . . And then I saw him climb a bench . . . Before the altar there . . . As though to look for Jesus and . . . Beseech His loving care . . . I watched him gently knock upon . . . The Tabernacle door . . . And I could almost hear The Voice . . . That he was listening for . . . But most of all I marveled at . . . This friendly little boy . . . Whose faith in God imbued him with . . . Such overwhelming joy . . . And then I knew that I could move . . . A mountain made of rock . . . If I just had the childish faith . . . That He would hear me knock.

God Has Time

God made the world in which we live . . . And He looks after it . . . As surely as He sees and weighs . . . The sins that we commit . . . And while He must be occupied . . . With many things each day . . . He never is too busy for . . . Whatever prayers we say . . . He never overlooks our thoughts . . . Or any deed we do . . . But He is always there to help . . . If we just ask Him to . . . He wants to guide us to our goal . . . And open every door . . . To everything of happiness . . . That we are striving for . . . God never is too busy to . . . Consider all our cares . . . Or in His wisdom and His might . . . To grant our fervent prayers.

Three Hail Marys

I whisper three Hail Marys when . . . My eyes behold the dawn . . . And when the shadows lengthen and . . . I know the day is gone . . . The first one tells my gratitude . . . The second asks for grace . . . The third implores a guiding hand . . . To help me fill my place . . . They are the special prayers I say . . . Each morning and each night . . . To overcome temptation and . . . To conquer every plight . . . To consecrate myself to God . . . Each moment of the day . . . And dwell in dreams of Heaven when . . . The sun has slipped away . . . I whisper three Hail Marys to . . . The Mary of my heart . . . That she will intercede for me . . . And we may never part.

Our Share of Blame

It is a human faculty . . . To make mistakes in life . . . And it is just as natural . . . To be involved in strife . . . And when these things occur despite . . . Our efforts to refrain . . . We may not have to bear the weight . . . Of every drop of rain . . . But human frailty does not . . . Entitle us to sin . . . For it is up to us to fight . . . And do our best to win . . . We cannot blame the weather or . . . The company we keep . . . Or try to tell almighty God . . . Our conscience was asleep . . . We have our mind for thinking and . . . Our will to act is free . . . And so the final score depends . . . On our sincerity.

Altar Boy

In cassock and in surplice white . . . He takes his privileged place . . . To serve the priest at Holy Mass . . . With reverence and grace . . . He kneels and stands with folded hands . . . And piously he shares . . . The Latin words and phrases of . . . Profound liturgic prayers . . . He moves the missal and the cloth . . . He sounds the altar chimes . . . And brings the wine and water at . . . The designated times . . . At Benediction he is there . . . To swing the censer high . . . And waft the fragrant incense to . . . The angels in the sky . . . He is the acolyte of God . . . Whose special time is spent . . . In serving Mass and being near . . . The Blessed Sacrament.

More Than a Smile

In friendship there is happiness . . . Surrounded by a smile . . . But also there are other things . . . That make this life worth while . . . In every friendship there is faith . . . And hope is kept alive . . . And there is that encouragement . . . On which we mortals thrive . . . It gives us inspiration and . . . The willingness to try . . . However difficult the task . . . Or overcast the sky . . . A friendship is a constant source . . . Of consolation true . . . Whenever anything goes wrong . . . And we are feeling blue . . . As long as we are loyal and . . . Avoid the sad mistake . . . Of giving nothing in return . . . For everything we take.

My Rosary

There is no other article . . . That means so much to me . . . Or gives me so much comfort as . . . My precious Rosary . . . Each bead is bright and lovely as . . . A flower or a gem . . . And sacred is the Crucifix . . . That watches over them . . . My fingers touch them lightly while . . . My head I gently nod . . . "Our Father" and "Hail Mary" and . . . The "Glory be to God" . . . I say my Rosary in church . . . At home and on retreat . . . I say it in my pocket when . . . I walk along the street . . . And when I quench the little flames . . . That light the candle-wicks . . . I always kneel beside my bed . . . And kiss the Crucifix.

God's Little Children

God surely loves the whole wide world . . . And blesses every part . . . But He must have a special place . . . For children in His heart . . . The little children who behold . . . The wonders of His earth . . . And whose imploring hands reach out . . . For merriment and mirth . . . To Him their gentle innocence . . . Is like a sparkling gem . . . And when they play or go to school . . . He watches over them . . . He follows them to supper and . . . He tucks them into bed . . . And fashions dreams from silver stars . . . To fill each sleepy head . . . Although God loves the whole wide world . . . And blesses every part . . . The little children surely hold . . . The center of His Heart.

Kitchen Prayer

Dear Lord, when I am cooking meals . . . I turn my thoughts to You . . . And ask You for Your gracious aid . . . In everything I do . . . I offer every morsel as . . . Another faithful prayer . . . And every wisp of oven smoke . . . As incense in the air . . . And when I wash the dishes and . . . I clean a pot or pan . . . I try with patience and with care . . . To do the best I can . . . The kitchen is my workshop but . . . It also is a place . . . Where I may tell my thoughts to You . . . And seek Your holy grace . . . Dear Lord, please help me with my task . . . That I may do my part . . . To serve my loving family . . . And please Your kindly heart.

Happy Birthday

A birthday is the time of life . . . When one more year is gone . . . A golden year that God allowed . . . To let us carry on . . . Indeed it is a compliment . . . To pass another mile . . . For God must feel our being here . . . Is somehow worth the while . . . And that is why I greet you and . . . Congratulate you too . . . But all the more because today . . . I know you as I do . . . Because you are a gentle soul . . . Forever good and kind . . . With only love and friendship in . . . Your noble heart and mind . . . And that is why I say a prayer . . . That God will always bless . . . Your life with joy on earth and with . . . Eternal happiness.

Faith, Hope and Charity

However much our worldly goods . . . Or prominence may be . . . The more important things are faith . . . And hope and charity . . . Our faith in God Whose power and . . . Whose glory great we know . . . Not through our human vision but . . . Because He tells us so . . . Our hope for perfect holiness . . . And sanctity of soul . . . And for the special grace to gain . . . Our everlasting goal . . . And last but not the least of all . . . Our willingness to love . . . Each high and humble neighbor and . . . Almighty God above . . . So let us pray and let us strive . . . For faith and hope anew . . . And charity to honor God . . . In everything we do.

Highest Calling

The highest calling in this world . . . Of struggle and of strife . . . Is that of undertaking the . . . Devout, religious life . . . To be a worthy priest of God . . . With all that it implies . . . For every Catholic, from his birth . . . Until the day he dies . . . To be a kind and gentle nun . . . Who gives her loving care . . . To children and their elders in . . . Their joy and their despair . . . Or else a humble brother who . . . Devotes his heart and soul . . . To special tasks that help the Church . . . Attain her every goal . . . There is no sacrifice so great . . . Or glorious today . . . As that of serving Jesus in . . . The true, religious way.

God Bless You

Dear friend of mine, there is no way . . . In which I could address you . . . With more sincerity of heart . . . Than just to say God bless you . . . My words could wish that all your cares . . . Would be a little lighter . . . And I could send you greeting cards . . . To make your hours brighter . . . My lips could call good luck to you . . . Or whisper happy landing . . . And I could promise you the depth . . . Of faithful understanding . . . But I am sure no other thought . . . Or message would impress you . . . As lovingly or lastingly . . . As asking God to bless you . . . And so I say God bless you, friend . . . In every good endeavor . . . And may His guiding grace be yours . . . Forever and forever.

Prayer to St. Anthony

St. Anthony, I pray to you . . . That you may help me find . . . The very special article . . . I lost or left behind . . . You are the guardian of goods . . . And in your loving care . . . I know that I may gain at last . . . The answer to my prayer . . . I really need this item and . . . It means so much to me . . . I want to get it back again . . . And keep it carefully . . . You are the patron saint of all . . . Who look for what is lost . . . Whatever be its size or weight . . . Its sentiment or cost . . . O good St. Anthony, I pray . . . That you will do your best . . . To help me find this article . . . And end my anxious quest.

Morning and Night

I say a prayer each morning and . . . I say one every night . . . Because somehow they make me feel . . . That everything is right . . . They seem to give the golden sun . . . A warm and friendly glow . . . And draw a brighter moonbeam to . . . The flowers and the snow . . . They sort of shape the silver stars . . . That twinkle in the sky . . . And give a breath of incense to . . . The winds that wander by . . . My morning and my evening prayers . . . Are candle-wicks that burn . . . So I may walk the proper path . . . And know which way to turn . . . And after all I love my God . . . And it is only right . . . That I should take the time to say . . . Good morning and good night.

Our Faith in God

Sometimes when things go wrong we think . . . Our prayers have been in vain . . . And frequently we are inclined . . . To murmur or complain . . . We feel that God has lost us in . . . The darkness of the night . . . Or maybe He has purposely . . . Ignored us in our plight . . . But that is not the way it is . . . However much it seems . . . Because our God is well aware . . . Of all our thoughts and dreams . . . And He will always listen to . . . Whatever prayers we say . . . However soft and silent and . . . However far away . . . But now and then as life goes on . . . He wants to try us out . . . To see if we have faith in Him . . . Or we are quick to doubt.

Think of Others

Consider not too much the things . . . That cause your heart to ache . . . But give a little of yourself . . . For some-one else's sake . . . Remember there are others who . . . Have troubles of their own . . . And in this world of selfish souls . . . They may be all alone . . . Sometimes it seems your cross in life . . . Is more than you can bear . . . And you incline to think that you . . . Are driven to despair . . . And yet if you will look around . . . Your eyes will surely see . . . That there are those who must endure . . . Far greater misery . . . Consider now the many hearts . . . That have a deeper ache . . . And do not feel too sorry for . . . Your less important sake.

I Would Be Good

Whenever we may meet, O God . . . I want to be prepared . . . To tell You that my only goods . . . Were those I always shared . . . To have a record that will show . . . A life of sacrifice . . . Without a selfish motive or . . . The naming of a price . . . I pray the world will say that I . . . Endeavored to be kind . . . Especially to all the poor . . . And all the lame and blind . . . For what is there to gain from greed . . . Or property amassed . . . And what will glory profit me . . . When I have breathed my last? . . . I only want to serve You, God . . . With all my heart and soul . . . And through Your mercy and Your love . . . To reach the highest goal.

My Sunday Prayers

Each Sunday when I go to church . . . I say a special prayer . . . For all my family and friends . . . And people everywhere . . . For those who help me to achieve . . . Each triumph over strife . . . And who inspire me to give . . . My very best in life . . . And if I have an enemy . . . I pray our feud will end . . . And I may have the happiness . . . To gain another friend . . . I give my gratitude to God . . . For blessings small and great . . . Including health and progress and . . . The food upon my plate . . . And as I contemplate the past . . . And all that now is gone . . . I ask forgiveness for my sins . . . And strength to carry on.

Ash Wednesday

Ash Wednesday is the day we start . . . The season that is Lent . . . When we are humble in our hearts . . . And given to repent . . . When ashes touch our foreheads and . . . We pray on bended knees . . . That God will take away our sins . . . And our iniquities . . . We contemplate our errors and . . . The weight of every vice . . . And dedicate ourselves to make . . . Some special sacrifice . . . And that is good and helpful and . . . Is pleasing to The Lord . . . But surely it does not deserve . . . A wonderful reward . . . For we should offer sacrifice . . . And for His mercy pray . . . Not just when Lenten season starts . . . But every night and day.

The Last Supper

Before Gethsemani He met . . . With His selected few . . . And He broke bread and drank with them . . . As gentle people do . . . But, more importantly, that night . . . His miracle was done . . . As He bestowed on us the gift . . . Of God's begotten Son . . . The twelve Apostles ate and sipped . . . Of holy bread and wine . . . Transformed into His Body and . . . His precious Blood divine . . . And then He gave this power to . . . His priests, from first to last . . . That they might reproduce and share . . . His Heavenly repast . . . In memory of how He died . . . Upon The Cross one day . . . To open God's great Kingdom and . . . To wash our sins away.

He Died for Me

They took my Lord and Saviour to . . . A hill called Calvary . . . And nailed Him to a wooden cross . . . For everyone to see . . . They crowned Him with a wreath of thorns . . . And pierced His gentle heart . . . And brazenly they mocked Him while . . . They watched His life depart . . . I was not there to witness it . . . Indeed I was not born . . . And yet I was a part of all . . . That cruelty and scorn . . . My sins condemned Him to His death . . . And nailed Him to the cross . . . And there He died to save me from . . . My soul's eternal loss . . . And I can only offer tears . . . Of deep sincerity . . . And thank my Lord and Saviour for . . . His cross on Calvary.

Holy Easter

Jerusalem was sleeping in . . . The hour of its dawn . . . While angels stood beside the grave . . . Where Jesus Christ was gone . . . The heavy stone was rolled away . . . The sepulchre was bare . . . While Simon Peter looked around . . . And Mary knelt in prayer . . . The Lord had risen from the death . . . He died on Calvary . . . And opened wide the sacred door . . . To His eternity . . . He washed away our mortal sins . . . And those of venial cast . . . That we might build a future on . . . Our errors of the past . . . So let us give our thanks to Him . . . And in our humble way . . . Attach ourselves to Jesus Christ . . . This holy Easter Day.

For You, My God

If ever I have wronged You, God . . . My heart is filled with tears . . . And I am sorry for the sins . . . Of all my foolish years . . . I beg forgiveness for the deeds . . . That weigh my weary soul . . . And humbly ask Your grace to reach . . . My everlasting goal . . . I want to follow in Your steps . . . And try to be like You . . . In every word I ever say . . . And everything I do . . . Because You are so merciful . . . And You have given me . . . The inspiration to attain . . . Your great eternity . . . I want to do the best I can . . . . In every way I know . . . And that is why I turn to You . . . Wherever I may go.

Immaculate Mary

O Mary, most immaculate . . . Help us be good and true . . . O Blessed Lady, pray for us . . . Who have recourse to you . . . We seldom hope for anything . . . We ever want or need . . . Unless we know your loving heart . . . Is there to intercede . . . Because you are Our Mother and . . . The Mother of Our Lord . . . And just a whispered word from you . . . Will bring His rich reward . . . We look to you for miracles . . . However great or small . . . Including His forgiveness when . . . We stumble and we fall . . . And through your most Immaculate Heart . . . We humbly hope and pray . . . That we may serve your gentle Son . . . And honor Him each day.

Our Contribution

Our contribution to the Church . . . Is in itself a prayer . . . Because it aids the Catholic cause . . . And people everywhere . . . It helps support our parishes . . . And all the good they do . . . And it provides for priests and nuns . . . And foreign missions too . . . And whether gold or silver or . . . The copper of a cent . . . No money could accomplish more . . . Or be more wisely spent . . . Our contribution paves a path . . . Of comfort for the poor . . . In sickness and in sorrow and . . . The hunger they endure . . . It is an act of charity . . . That brings its own reward . . . And speaks the word of eloquence . . . That gratifies The Lord.

Your Blessing

Your blessing, God, is like a gift . . . Of silver and of gold . . . And sometimes it is almost more . . . Than I have strength to hold . . . Sometimes You shower so much joy . . . And happiness on me . . . That life is like a paradise . . . Of perfect ecstasy . . . And that is why I do not mind . . . The lightning and the rain . . . Or any hail or thunderbolt . . . That shakes my window-pane . . . I have my disappointments and . . . My share of earthly grief . . . But always I remember, God . . . That there is some relief . . . Because when I have said my prayer . . . I hear Your soft reply. . . And when I lift my eyes I see . . . A rainbow in the sky.

Jesus, My Shepherd

Dear Jesus, I am still too small . . . To really understand . . . Please let me put my tiny heart . . . In Your beloved hand . . . I want to be the little lamb . . . That nestles in Your arms . . . Away from sin and sadness and . . . From everything that harms . . . I never want to leave Your side . . . For any kind of play . . . Because You are so good to me . . . Each moment of the day . . . I know You are my Father in . . . The Heaven of my dreams . . . Where everything is beautiful . . . And happy as it seems . . . Dear Jesus, be my Shepherd now . . . Protect and comfort me . . . And let me be Your little lamb . . . For all eternity.

Never in Vain

No worthy deed is all in vain . . . However small or brief . . . For it must bring some happiness . . . Or offer some relief . . . At least it is a gentle thought . . . And very probably . . . It sets a good example for . . . Promoting charity . . . It may receive no gratitude . . . In fact it may be spurned . . . And yet it benefits and leaves . . . A lesson to be learned . . . A worthy deed in life reflects . . . A sympathetic hand . . . That holds a certain willingness . . . To care and understand . . . And though it may not be enough . . . To overcome the rain . . . No worthy deed sincerely done . . . Is ever all in vain.

My Valentine for You

My valentine for you today . . . Is this my heartfelt prayer . . . That good St. Valentine will bless . . . And keep you in his care . . . That he will guide and comfort you . . . And help in every task . . . And intercede with God for all . . . The favors you may ask . . . I pray that he will light your path . . . With sunshine every day . . . And keep the shrouds and shadows and . . . The little tears away . . . Because you are so noble and . . . So generous and true . . . That I sincerely wish the best . . . Of everything for you . . . And so with all the feeling in . . . This grateful heart of mine . . . I offer this petition as . . . My loving valentine.

Prayer for Humility

Help me, O God, to know and fight . . . The faults there are in me . . . Including every part of greed . . . And petty jealousy . . . Let not my tongue say idle words . . . Or tell the smallest lie . . . And let me not complain of rain . . . Or weep and wonder why . . . O God, enable me to grow . . . In wisdom and in grace . . . That I may always recognize . . . And keep my humble place . . . Because I want to live my life . . . According to Your way . . . To honor You and try to do . . . Some worthy deed each day . . . I want to be considerate . . . Of others everywhere . . . And fashion every moment to . . . The pattern of a prayer.

God in My Heart

I used to think that Sunday was . . . The only day to pray . . . And give my God the gratitude . . . I felt inclined to say . . . Until one day I met a friend . . . Who showed me I was wrong . . . And how to follow in His steps . . . And keep my courage strong . . . My friend reminded me that I . . . Could do my daily task . . . And even as I labored I . . . Could move my lips to ask . . . That I could offer silent thanks . . . And say a fervent prayer . . . And never once neglect my work . . . Or fail to do my share . . . And now I know it matters not . . . How wearily I plod . . . For while the hand is occupied . . . The heart may speak to God.

My Contrition

Forgive me, God, for all the sins . . . Which I would now confess . . . And give me grace to start anew . . . In holy happiness . . . I am contrite because I know . . . If I do not repent . . . You will be angry with me, and . . . I fear my punishment . . . But also I am sorry, God . . . And I present my plea . . . Because each day in every way . . . You are so good to me . . . Because I know that every time . . . I do a wrong to You . . . I show I am ungrateful and . . . I hurt You through and through . . . O gracious God, please hear me and . . . Forgive my every sin . . . I promise to be better now . . . Than I have ever been.

Lord, Help Me Serve

Lord, help me give myself today . . . To those who need me most . . . Without desire for reward . . . And never any boast . . . Teach me to live for others and . . . To try my best to be . . . As good and kind to them as I . . . Would have them be to me . . . Because I want the outcome of . . . Each task I undertake . . . To be a bit of happiness . . . For someone else's sake . . . I want to serve my neighbor and . . . The stranger on the street . . . In every manner that may tend . . . To make their lives complete . . . Help me, O Lord, to give myself . . . With all my heart and soul . . . To everyone who strives to gain . . . That everlasting goal.

O Holy Trinity

O God The Father and The Son . . . And God The Holy Ghost . . . I praise You in Your kingdom great . . . And in The Sacred Host . . . With all my heart I do believe . . . This wondrous mystery . . . As I adore and I implore . . . The Holy Trinity . . . I love You, God The Father, and . . . I want to do Your will . . . I love You, God The Son, and pledge . . . Each promise to fulfill . . . I love You, God The Holy Ghost . . . And I look up to You . . . For all the wisdom and the strength . . . To see my struggles through . . . However high or humble or . . . How average I may be . . . I will be ever grateful to . . . The Holy Trinity.

The Catholic's Prayer

God bless our Holy Father in . . . The Vatican at Rome . . . God bless our noble priests and nuns . . . And every Catholic home . . . Endow the Church with prominence . . . And everything it needs . . . To spread the gospel and the truth . . . With kind and worthy deeds . . . Give greater wisdom to our press . . . And every Catholic tongue . . . And magnify each echo when . . . Our sacred songs are sung . . . God bless our missions that extend . . . Beyond the seven seas . . . And multiply our convents and . . . Our universities . . . God bless the Church and everyone . . . Who is a part of it . . . That it may grow and all the world . . . May know and benefit.

On Your Ordination

On this your ordination day . . . I offer prayers for you . . . And thank Our Lord for having made . . . Your sweetest dream come true . . . I pray that you will grow in grace . . . And gather holy fame . . . To edify the priesthood and . . . To glorify His name . . . May you enjoy the best of health . . . And may each Mass you say . . . Provide the inspiration for . . . A fruitful Catholic day . . . May words of wisdom sanctify . . . The sermons that you preach . . . And may your tongue convince the world . . . Of every truth you teach . . . God bless you and protect your soul . . . Through struggle and through strife . . . And may you persevere and live . . . A long and priestly life.

My Holy Communion

When I approach the altar and . . . I kneel before the rail . . . The pleasures of the world appear . . . So empty and so pale . . . Because the power of the priest . . . Has touched infinity . . . And in a moment he will share . . . His miracle with me . . . I dwell in reverence and awe . . . And marvel as I think . . . That Christ's own Blood and Body are . . . To be my food and drink . . . And when I have received The Host . . . And I begin to pray . . . I cannot look at anything . . . Or keep my tears away . . . My tears of sorrow for the sins . . . For which He sacrificed . . . And all the tears of ecstasy . . . In joy with Jesus Christ.

Before the Crucifix

Behold, O Jesus sweet and kind . . . I humbly bend my knee . . . And beg to be imbued with faith . . . And hope and charity . . . In sorrow over all my sins . . . My soul is filled with grief . . . And firmly I intend to turn . . . A new and brighter leaf . . . To make amends for every wrong . . . That I have done to You . . . And sanctify my life on earth . . . With everything I do . . . Because You are so good to me . . . And You have suffered so . . . While I am not deserving of . . . The blessings You bestow . . . I memorize what David said . . . In true, prophetic tones . . . "They pierced my hands and feet and they . . . Have numbered all my bones."

First Little Prayer

O Jesus dear, I love You so . . . With all my tiny heart . . . And now that You and I have met . . . Please, never let us part . . . My parents introduced us, and . . . The priest and sister too . . . Have told me Who You are and why . . . I owe so much to You . . . You are The Infant Jesus Who . . . Was born on Christmas Day . . . And Who is always watching when . . . I sleep or when I play . . . You smile when I am really good . . . And cry when I am bad . . . And, oh, dear Jesus, I would like . . . To keep You always glad . . . I love You and I promise You . . . That I will try to be . . . Your faithful and devoted child . . . For all eternity.

Keep the Faith

Along the open lanes of life . . . And far behind its walls . . . Forever keep the faith, my friend . . . No matter what befalls . . . Forever put your trust in God . . . And all your confidence . . . In Catholic courage and the gift . . . Of childish innocence . . . Be loyal to the Church and those . . . Who walk the holy way . . . However much your hopes may dim . . . Or it may rain today . . . Let not temptation blind your eyes . . . Or bind your hands and feet . . . Heed not the foolish phrases of . . . The fallacies you meet . . . Whatever magic moves the mind . . . To something strange or odd . . . Forever keep the faith, my friend . . . And give yourself to God.

To Our Lady of Fatima

Our Lady of the Rosary . . . Look down with loving grace . . . And bless the world with harmony . . . For every land and race . . . Unite our hearts as one with you . . . And let our battles cease . . . That we may have the miracle . . . Of everlasting peace . . . At Fatima your wonders and . . . Your wishes were revealed . . . And there you promised that our prayers . . . Would be our strongest shield . . . We kiss the holy Crucifix . . . And hopefully we hold . . . The little beads and those on which . . . The Mysteries are told . . . We pray for freedom and for calm . . . Beyond the farthest sea . . . And so that some day all the world . . . May say the Rosary.

Our Only Task

As long as we believe in God . . . He will not let us down . . . No matter what our loneliness . . . Or reason for renown . . . As long as we are true to Him . . . And try to do our best . . . We may be confident that all . . . Our efforts will be blest . . . For that is all that God demands . . . Or hopes that we will give . . . According to the way of life . . . That humans ought to live . . . He wants us to remember Him . . . And seek His loving care . . . By just a moment now and then . . . Devoted to a prayer . . . And just by doing all we can . . . To conquer every fear . . . And giving Him our heartfelt praise . . . And gratitude sincere.

You Heard My Prayer

Dear God, with all my humble heart . . . I thank You fervently . . . Because You granted the request . . . That meant so much to me . . . You heard my prayer and answered it . . . In Your most gracious way . . . And thereby You fulfilled the wish . . . I whispered on that day . . . Oh, I have asked You many times . . . To help me gain some goal . . . And You have poured Your blessings down . . . Upon my grateful soul . . . But this was something special and . . . It meant a great deal more . . . Than many gifts or favors I . . . Had asked of You before . . . And so I say this prayer of thanks . . . And promise faithfully . . . To try to be deserving of . . . Your generosity.

Flower of Life

I bought a pretty vase today . . . And put it on a shelf . . . To hold the lovely flowers that . . . I gather for myself . . . The hollyhock and hyacinth . . . The lilac and the rose . . . The tulip and forget-me-not . . . And every kind that grows . . . And some of them will blossom forth . . . And some of them will die . . . As I may gather joy in life . . . Or merely sit and sigh . . . A flower is a symbol of . . . The life we live today . . . And whether we are flourishing . . . Or we would waste away . . . And whether we respond to all . . . The kindly care we get . . . Or shrivel up in selfishness . . . And languish in regret.

Guide Me, O Lord

O Lord, I want to serve You well . . . In everything I do . . . That my example may invite . . . Another soul to You . . . Please help me be dependable . . . And honest and sincere . . . Without a trace of vanity . . . And never any fear . . . Endow me with a civil tongue . . . And with a Christian mind . . . And teach me how to smile and to . . . Be tolerant and kind . . . Guide every step I take, O Lord . . . In darkness and in light . . . That I may wander not by day . . . Or lose my way at night . . . Help me to plan tomorrow and . . . Reflect on what is past . . . And with Your grace enable me . . . To persevere at last.

Believe in God

There will be times when you are sad . . . And know not what to do . . . And when you tell yourself there is . . . No thought to comfort you . . . But just remember this, my friend . . . That God is everywhere . . . And all you ever have to do . . . Is say a little prayer . . . For He is right beside you and . . . He hears each word you say . . . And He decides the weather and . . . The fortune of the day . . . He is your everlasting friend . . . In time of need or stress . . . And only He can give you tears . . . Or bring you happiness . . . So trust in God with all your heart . . . And tell Him that you care . . . For He will gladly listen, friend . . . And heed your smallest prayer.

Spiritual Bouquet

I send your heart this holy gift . . . To help your dreams come true . . . A fond novena offering . . . Especially for you . . . A spiritual bouquet of love . . . For every day of nine . . . To sanctify your soul anew . . . And give you grace divine . . . To light the skies around your day . . . Wherever you may be . . . And crown your night with silver stars . . . To keep you company . . . Each day of nine my prayers will ask . . . For blessings of the best . . . To guide your progress and to make . . . Your heart the happiest . . . May you attain the greatest goal . . . In everything you do . . . May you have peace and comfort and . . . May God be good to you.

God First

Our first responsibility . . . Is unto God above . . . Far greater than to our pursuit . . . Of labor, play or love . . . Far more than to the glory and . . . The fame we would achieve . . . Or any earthly principle . . . In which we might believe . . . For all of our possessions and . . . The very life we live . . . Are basically the benefits . . . That only God can give . . . Without His help we could not speak . . . Or walk or lift a hand . . . Or have the human mind to think . . . And try to understand . . . Our family and country have . . . Their places on this sod . . . But first we owe our homage and . . . Our gratitude to God.

The Angelus

I hear the Angelus ring out . . . Each morning, noon and night . . . And everything of life becomes . . . More beautiful and bright . . . The Angel of The Lord is there . . . And Mary bows her head . . . In humble recognition of . . . The message that is said . . . Each day I listen to her words . . . And cherish every one . . . "Behold the handmaid of The Lord . . . And may Your will be done" . . . And so the miracle was wrought . . . And there was born a Child . . . While king and shepherd knelt in awe . . . And holy angels smiled . . . I hear the Angelus ring out . . . And softly fade away . . . And in my heart I know The Lord . . . Has blest another day.

My Humble Thanks

This prayer, O Lord, is not to ask . . . For anything on earth . . . But just to give my humble thanks . . . For what they may be worth . . . I thank You for the sunshine and . . . The stars that fill the sky . . . And for the rain that quenches thirst . . . When everything is dry . . . For family and friendship and . . . The stranger on the street . . . The glory of a triumph and . . . The lesson of defeat . . . The beauty of a flower and . . . The sweetness of a song . . . And for the mercy You have shown . . . When I have done a wrong . . . I thank You, Lord, for every joy . . . And for my sorrow too . . . And for the hope and vision of . . . Eternal life with You.

In Life and Death

O God, Who grants all life on earth . . . Hear now my humble prayer . . . That I may be forever in . . . Your kind and loving care . . . That I may trace the pattern of . . . Your angels and Your saints . . . And be prepared and willing to . . . Abide by Your restraints . . . I long to leave this world at last . . . Without a touch of fear . . . But with the faith and confidence . . . That You are always near . . . I know that life from day to day . . . Was never meant to last . . . And some time I must say goodby . . . And melt into the past . . . O God, Who rules the destiny . . . Of every dream and breath . . . Allow my soul to live for You . . . And die a holy death.

The Ten Commandments

I *I am the Lord thy God;*
thou shalt not have strange gods before me.

II *Thou shalt not take the name of the Lord thy God in vain.*

III *Remember thou keep holy the Lord's day.*

IV *Honor thy father and thy mother.*

V *Thou shalt not kill.*

VI *Thou shalt not commit adultery.*

VII *Thou shalt not steal.*

VIII *Thou shalt not bear false witness against thy neighbor.*

IX *Thou shalt not covet thy neighbor's wife.*

X *Thou shalt not covet thy neighbor's goods.*

The First Commandment

Give homage to your Lord and God . . . Bow down before His throne . . . For He is mighty over all . . . And He is God alone . . . Look not upon an idol or . . . An image in the sun . . . And worship not the moon or stars . . . Or how the rivers run . . . Serve not another master on . . . The earth or in the sky . . . Kneel not before a graven thing . . . Or shadows passing by . . . For God is vengeful unto those . . . Who recognize Him not . . . And those who dare to hate Him and . . . Who blame Him for their lot . . . But He is filled with love for all . . . Who walk upon this sod . . . And who adore and praise Him as . . . Their true and only God.

The Second Commandment

Take not the name of God in vain . . . In anger or in jest . . . Or any disrespectful way . . . That it may be expressed . . . His name is ever sacred and . . . It should not touch the air . . . Except with humble reverence . . . As in a fervent prayer . . . But you should say it when you kneel . . . And ask His blessing great . . . Or His forgiveness for the sins . . . You seek to expiate . . . Be thoughtful and be cautious how . . . The name of God is used . . . And never say it carelessly . . . Or let it be abused . . . It is a privilege to invoke . . . His everlasting name . . . And they who speak in disrespect . . . Must bear the dreadful blame.

The Third Commandment

God made the heaven and the earth . . . The seas that ebb and flow . . . The sun and moon, the silver stars . . . And all the winds that blow . . . Six days He labored at His task . . . And then He chose to rest . . . And thus His Third Commandment was . . . Indelibly impressed . . . The seventh day He set aside . . . For us to take our ease . . . To honor Him, enjoy our dreams . . . And dwell in memories . . . It is the holy sabbath and . . . The day that we should spend . . . In leisure with our family . . . Alone or with a friend . . . It is the time to leave our tools . . . And put our work away . . . While humbly and with grateful hearts . . . We go to church and pray.

The Fourth Commandment

Obey and love your parents and . . . Respect the words they say . . . Who do so much to care for you . . . And guide you on your way . . . Give ear to them and do their will . . . Wherever you may be . . . And share with them your every deed . . . And every memory . . . For it is God's commandment great . . . To honor and revere . . . The father and the mother who . . . Are always near and dear . . . Speak well of them to all the world . . . Sincerely and with pride . . . Your kind and loving guardians . . . Against whatever tide . . . And when the sun is going down . . . Upon their smiles and tears . . . Remember and take care of them . . . In their remaining years.

The Fifth Commandment

Almighty God created life . . . And it is His to end . . . With all the noble virtues and . . . The evils it may blend . . . And it is not for us to say . . . How long the time or brief . . . No matter what our weariness . . . Or poignancy of grief . . . No one may take another's life . . . Or trifle with his own . . . For each immortal soul belongs . . . To God, and God alone . . No merciful or vengeful scheme . . . Can ever justify . . . The deed that would determine when . . . The body has to die . . . We have no right to end our plight . . . And no excuse to slay . . . But only God, Who made the world . . . May take its life away.

The Sixth Commandment

Seek not the pleasures of this world . . . Whatever they may be . . . But follow faithfully the path . . . To God's eternity . . . Keep all your actions and your thoughts . . . Immaculate and whole . . . Let no unchaste desire stain . . . Your everlasting soul . . . However strong your body is . . . It must return to dust . . . And dire punishment awaits . . . Immodesty and lust . . . But God rewards the virtuous . . . Who always strive to win . . . And overcome temptation that . . . Would lead them into sin . . . The innocent and spotless soul . . . Is God's own counterpart . . . And in His angels and His saints . . . God loves the pure of heart.

The Seventh Commandment

The Lord commands you not to take . . . And hold unto yourself . . . The goods and chattels that belong . . . On someone else's shelf . . . However much or little you . . . Acquire and conceal . . . The Lord has spoken and has said . . . It is a sin to steal . . . And if you cheat another of . . . His progress or his fame . . . Or filch the credit he is due . . . The evil is the same . . . For his possessions are his right . . . To treasure and retain . . . And no one is entitled to . . . Deprive him of his gain . . . Now, therefore, be content to count . . . The things that are your own . . . Respect your fellowman and leave . . . His property alone.

The Eighth Commandment

The Eighth Commandment cautions us . . . Against the smallest lie . . . That it may not disgrace the soul . . . When we are come to die . . . It warns us all to tell the truth . . . No matter what our shame . . . Or how it hurts us to accept . . . The burden of our blame . . . Because to bear false witness is . . . A very serious sin . . . Against our Maker and against . . . Our neighbor and our kin . . . And there is no deceit in life . . . That does not bring dismay . . . For God is jealous of the truth . . . According to His way . . . And only by the words we speak . . . And by the deeds we do . . . Can we present our honesty . . . And prove that we are true.

The Ninth Commandment

Gaze not upon your neighbor's wife . . . Nor seek in reverie . . . Another distant creature who . . . Is beautiful as she . . . Desire not companionship . . . That God denies to you . . . But keep your heart where it belongs . . . And be forever true . . . Remember God's commandment well . . . And let His will be done . . . That no one put asunder now . . . Whom He has joined as one . . . Be mindful of the blessings that . . . Are yours to have and hold . . . And all that life is promising . . . To fashion and unfold . . . And be content to go your way . . . With happiness and pride . . . And loving gratitude to her . . . Who never leaves your side.

The Tenth Commandment

Desire not your neighbor's house . . . His chattels or estate . . . Nor contemplate his place in life . . . With jealousy and hate . . . Begrudge him not the glory or . . . The fruits of his success . . . And be not envious of him . . . For any happiness . . . Because it is The Lord's decree . . . For every soul to heed . . . And there is nothing to be gained . . . From avarice and greed . . . Be grateful for your blessings now . . . And pray to God for more . . . But do not covet anything . . . Beyond your neighbor's door . . . For what is his belongs to him . . . And yours belongs to you . . . And each shall harvest to his own . . . Of what he strives to do.